The Patient Griselda

David Murray Smith

Kessinger Publishing's Rare Reprints

Thousands of Scarce and Hard-to-Find Books on These and other Subjects!

- Americana
- Ancient Mysteries
- Animals
- Anthropology
- Architecture
- Arts
- Astrology
- Bibliographies
- Biographies & Memoirs
- Body, Mind & Spirit
- Business & Investing
- Children & Young Adult
- Collectibles
- Comparative Religions
- Crafts & Hobbies
- Earth Sciences
- Education
- Ephemera
- Fiction
- Folklore
- Geography
- Health & Diet
- History
- Hobbies & Leisure
- Humor
- Illustrated Books
- Language & Culture
- Law
- Life Sciences

- Literature
- Medicine & Pharmacy
- Metaphysical
- Music
- Mystery & Crime
- Mythology
- Natural History
- Outdoor & Nature
- Philosophy
- Poetry
- Political Science
- Science
- Psychiatry & Psychology
- Reference
- Religion & Spiritualism
- Rhetoric
- Sacred Books
- Science Fiction
- Science & Technology
- Self-Help
- Social Sciences
- Symbolism
- Theatre & Drama
- Theology
- Travel & Explorations
- War & Military
- Women
- Yoga
- *Plus Much More!*

We kindly invite you to view our catalog list at:
http://www.kessinger.net

THIS ARTICLE WAS EXTRACTED FROM THE BOOK:

Tales of Chivalry and Romance

BY THIS AUTHOR:

David Murray Smith

ISBN 0766189104

READ MORE ABOUT THE BOOK AT OUR WEB SITE:

http://www.kessinger.net

OR ORDER THE COMPLETE
BOOK FROM YOUR FAVORITE STORE

ISBN 0766189104

Because this article has been extracted from a parent book, it may have non-pertinent text at the beginning or end of it.

Any blank pages following the article are necessary for our book production requirements. The article herein is complete.

THE PATIENT GRISELDA.

(THE CLERK'S TALE FROM CHAUCER.)

FAR in the west of Italy, spreading away from the lofty snow-covered Mount Vesulas, expands the rich plain of Saluce, yellow with waving fields of wheat and corn, green with vineyards, and overlooked by many a tower and town founded in ages long gone past. The Marquis Walter, the descendant of a line of sovereigns, ruled this land in peace and prosperity; for all his subjects, his lords as well as his

34 TALES OF CHIVALRY AND ROMANCE.

humbler people, were loyal and content, and regarded their ruler with love for his goodness and dread for his authority. Of all the princes of Lombardy the marquis was of the highest lineage and most gentle birth. He was young, strong, and noble in presence, and was a pattern of honour and of courtesy; and, though too steadfast and determined in carrying out his own will, he could wisely guide his country. Indeed he managed the affairs of his realm more discreetly than the affairs which more nearly concerned his own person. For himself, he followed the pleasures or the whims of the moment without thinking or caring what might happen in the future. He sported with hounds and hawks all over his dominion, and troubled himself little with the time to come. But, worst of all, he would on no account be persuaded to take a wife; and, as he was the last of his race, his subjects were in dread lest their country should pass into the hands of a stranger who might oppress and rob them, and change their fertile plains into battle-fields.

About this matter the people became so anxious, that on a certain day a number of them came before the marquis, and one of them, the wisest of all the people, thus addressed him :—

"O noble Marquis," said he, "your love for the people emboldens us to tell you of our distresses and

THE PATIENT GRISELDA. 35

our fears whenever misfortune threatens us. Let it please you now that we make our complaint to you with vexed hearts, and let your ears not disdain my voice. It is certain, my lord, that your people love you so well, and delight so much in your government, that they cannot imagine how they could live more happily than under your rule. One thing only do we desire. Were you but a wedded man, then your people would be indeed completely happy. For the yoke of marriage is not a yoke of service but of sovereignty. You marry to be a master, not a slave. And let it be among your wise thoughts that time is passing, and that whether we are sleeping or waking, walking or riding, time is ever flying, and will wait for no man, And though you are still flourishing in green youth, yet age is always silently drawing near. And at any age death may come; for though we all know that we must die, none knows at what time that will happen. Accept of advice from us who have ever been ready to receive your commands; and, if you agree, we will choose for you a wife, born of the highest and gentlest lineage in the land, that we may do you honour to the best of our wisdom. Marry then, and relieve us from our dread; for if it so should happen that by your death your name should be lost, and a strange successor should seize upon

36   TALES OF CHIVALRY AND ROMANCE.

your heritage, surely woe would be the fate of your people."

The meek prayers and the sad aspect of the multitude melted the heart of the marquis.

"You would persuade me, my people," said he, "to do a thing I have never thought about. I have rejoiced in my liberty. I have been free; but there is no freedom in marriage. Nevertheless, I know you are sincere, and I trust in your wisdom as I have ever done. Wherefore I agree to marry as soon as I may. But one thing I must demand. You have offered to choose me a wife. I relieve you from that trouble. High lineage cannot always be trusted to, for children are often unlike their fathers. Goodness comes from heaven and not from parentage, therefore I leave in heaven's hands the ordering of my marriage and of my good fortune and estate. Let me alone in choosing my wife—that duty I shall take upon myself. But I charge you upon your lives to give me assurance that whatever wife I take, ye will reverence and obey her throughout your lives, in word and deed, here and everywhere, as if she were an emperor's daughter. And more, you must here swear to me never to complain against or resist my choice. For since, at your request, I am to lose my liberty and be married, then, as I live, I will marry her on whom I set my

THE PATIENT GRISELDA.

heart. And if ye do not agree to this, then I pray you speak no more of marrying me, for I will remain a bachelor!"

Then they all heartily agreed to what the marquis proposed, and vowed that whomever he might choose, be she rich or poor, high or low, they would not dispute his choice, but would reverence her and loyally serve her, as though she were the daughter of an emperor. But fearing that the marquis might forget his promise, and refuse to marry after all, the people besought him to fix upon a day for the wedding feast. At their request, Marquis Walter stated the day on which he would be married; and the people, kneeling humbly before him, rendered him thanks before they went their way. Meantime the marquis commands his officers, and his knights, and squires to prepare the wedding feast; and soon the palace is busy with those that move to and fro continually providing for the appointed day.

Not far from the noble palace of the Marquis of Saluce was a small village that nestled among rich fields and woods. Here dwelt a number of poor people—shepherds and husbandmen, whose simple wants were supplied by the bounty of the soil and the pastures. Among these humble villagers, the poorest of them all was Janicula, who lived in a hut with his daughter Griselda. This maid was the most beautiful in all the land, and her mind and heart were as pure as her face was lovely. She had been poorly nurtured, and knew not what luxury was. She drank

only of the well, and the fruits and the grain of the fields yielded her simple food. And though Griselda was but very young, she was of a wise and sober dis-

THE PATIENT GRISELDA. 39

position. With great reverence and love did she pro
vide for her father's wants, labouring early and late,
and never being idle except only when she slept. And
when she came home at twilight from herding her few
sheep in the fields, she brought with her nourishing
roots and herbs, from which she prepared a simple
meal for her father and herself. Her daily work was
hard, and hard was the bed upon which she lay down
at nightfall; but so sweet and patient was her nature,
that she was contented with her lot, and devoted herself with all reverence and diligence to keep her
old father cheerful, and to see that he wanted for
nothing.

Upon this poor, simple Griselda, the marquis, as he
rode hunting through the village, had often looked with
admiration. But not thoughtlessly or foolishly did the
Lord of Saluce regard the poor village girl. He saw
that her nature was sweet, serious, and cheerful; he
knew that she was faithful, full of virtue and goodness;
and he resolved that, if he should ever marry, he would
marry her and her only.

And now the day appointed for the wedding had
come, and there was a great wondering at the palace
among all the lords and officers, who the lady might
be that the marquis had decided to marry. But no
one could tell; and many said, "Why will not our
marquis forsake his vanity and foolishness? Why

40   TALES OF CHIVALRY AND ROMANCE.

does he thus continue to deceive himself and us?"
For many thought that there would be no marriage
after all.

Meantime the marquis caused rich brooches and
rings, and gems set in blue and gold, to be made
for his bride, as well as splendid apparel. On the
morning of the wedding day, all the palace—hall and
chamber—was fitted out as for a great rejoicing, and
the store-rooms were bursting with plenty. The lords
and ladies were gaily attired for the wedding; but
no one among them yet knew who was to be the
bride.

Then forth came the marquis, royally dressed, and,
followed by the courtiers and great ladies, he rode
to the little village where Griselda dwelt. Poor Griselda, little thinking that all this great array was for
her sake alone, had gone forth with another maiden
to fetch water from the well when she heard the
sound of music, and, looking up, she saw the noble
company coming towards the village.

She went home from the well as soon as she could,
for she knew this was the day the Marquis of Saluce
was to be married, and she wished to see the proces-
sion.

"I will stand in our door," she said, "with other
village maidens that are my companions, and see the

marchioness. And I will be diligent that I may finish the work that I have to do, and so have leisure to see the great lady as she rides to the palace."

But she had scarce got back from the well to her

own door with the pitcher of water, when the marquis called her by her name. Griselda turned, set down

42   TALES OF CHIVALRY AND ROMANCE.

the pitcher, and, falling upon her knees, she listened with serious countenance to know what were the commands of the marquis.

The marquis spoke to the village girl with a grave and sober countenance, but with a kindly voice.

"Where is your father, Griselda?" asked he.

"Lord Walter, he is here now," she answered with humble mien.

Griselda then went into the hut without delay, and brought forth her father, Janicula.

Then the marquis, coming forward, took the old man's hand, and taking him aside—

"Janicula," said he, "I can no longer hide the delight of my heart. If you will grant me your consent, I will marry your daughter, and she shall be my wife to the end of her life. I know you are my faithful subject, and that whatever pleases me you will consent to. But tell me now faithfully, as you would tell me if I were not your prince, will you take me for your son-in-law?"

So suddenly had this wonderful thing happened, that the poor peasant Janicula was struck with amazement and fear. He blushed, and stood quaking and abashed. Scarce could he utter a word.

"Lord," said Janicula, "your will is my will. Against your will I cannot wish anything. You are

THE PATIENT GRISELDA. 43

my dear sovereign. Arrange this matter then as you desire."

"Let us go into your dwelling,—you, and your daughter, and I," said the marquis to the old man; "for I wish to ask her if she is willing to be my wife, to love and to obey me. All this shall be done in your presence ; for I shall not speak to Griselda but in your hearing."

Then all the people came round about the hut, wondering at the tenderness of Griselda, and praising her for her faithful love and care of her father. But Griselda's wonder was far greater than theirs, for never before had she seen such a brave sight. Never before had such a guest entered her hut ; and as she looked at him her face became pale with excitement and with fear.

When the Marquis of Saluce entered with the old man by the door of the hut into the only room which the miserable dwelling of Janicula contained, the latter, as was the custom, knelt down on the floor, and the Marquis, calling to Griselda and taking her hand in his, in a gentle and winning voice said :—

"Griselda, your father has given me his consent to marry you, and now I must ask you if you are willing to become my wife. Are you ready with a willing heart to agree ? Are you willing, whether you ever

TALES OF CHIVALRY AND ROMANCE.

be merry or sad. to be obedient to me, and to do whatever I wish, and never to complain? When I say 'yes,' you must never say 'no,' nor whatever I wish you to do must you ever refuse, or even wear a frowning or complaining countenance. Promise me this, and I will make you my wife."

Trembling with fear, and amazed at what she had heard, Griselda answered :—

"My lord, I am unworthy of the honour to which you invite me. But as your will is so is mine; and here I swear that never in deed or thought will I disobey you, even though you should bid me die."

"It is enough, my own Griselda!" said the marquis.

Then he went to the door, and looked upon his people with grave and serious countenance.

"This is my wife that stands here," said he, taking Griselda by the hand. "Honour and love her every one of you that loves me."

Soon he ordered the ladies of his court to clothe Griselda in the splendid attire which he had commanded to be prepared. And the great ladies, who were not very willing to touch the plain, rude clothes in which she was clad, were obliged to obey their ruler. They took off all her peasant dress, and clothed her anew from head to foot in royal robes. They combed out her hair, and with their dainty fingers they placed a crown of gold upon her head.

GRISELDA ACCEPTS THE MARQUIS.

46 TALES OF CHIVALRY AND ROMANCE.

Her garments were clasped with golden clasps, and her breast shone with jewels and precious stones; and when she was brought forth to the people, she was so much changed by being clad in such glorious array that they scarcely recognised her.

Then the marquis married her, placing a ring of gold upon her finger; and afterwards seating her on a snow-white horse, he set out with her to his palace followed by crowds of joyous people, and spent the day in high revelry until the sinking of the sun.

And this Marchioness Griselda was so highly gifted and so graceful, that no one would ever have thought she was born in a poor hut and rudely reared; for she seemed so noble in presence, and was also so wise and kind in manner, that it seemed rather she had been reared in a palace than a cot. A little while and every one that looked in her face loved her—she was so virtuous, so winning in manner, so full of goodness, so wise and kind. And not only in the land of Saluce was she spoken of with praise, but her fame was known in many regions, and many a one travelled to Saluce only to look upon her.

And now the Marquis Walter, after his royal wedding was over, dwelt in peace and ease in his palace. He had seen that virtue might be found in the huts of the humble; he was proud of his wife; and he became more and more dear to his people, who now knew

THE PATIENT GRISELDA.

that he was a prudent man. And well might he be proud of Griselda, for not only was she well-skilled in all housewife's matters, but she promoted the common good of the people, and there was no discord or strife in the country that she could not, with her wisdom, appease. If the marquis, her husband, was absent when quarrels broke forth in the state, she stilled the strife with her wise words and her fair judgment, and reconciled those that were at enmity.

A year had passed after the marriage of the marquis with Griselda, when a little daughter was born to them. The child was still an infant when a violent desire to try the constancy of his wife and prove whether she would keep the vow she made at her marriage, never to gainsay his wish whatever he might do, entered into the marquis's heart. But why should he put her to trial? He had proved her love and her constancy and obedience, and had ever found her in all things willing to do his will cheerfully; but whether it was her mild patience that provoked him to tempt her to disobey, or whether it was that he might know how really good she was, I cannot tell. This was the manner in which he tried her truth.

One night when she was alone he came to her with stern and troubled face.

"Griselda," said he, "you have not forgotten the day I took you from your wretched hut, and raised you to a state of high nobility. I do not think the high rank that I have raised you to makes you forgetful of the low estate in which I found you. Take

heed, then, of every word I say to you—no one hears but us two. Though you are dear to me, you are not beloved by my nobles. They say it is an insult to them to be made subject to you, and to serve you—born as you were in a poor hut. And they have said

THE PATIENT GRISELDA. 49

this openly since your daughter was born. For my part, I desire not to offend my nobles. I must live in peace, and in friendship with them, as I have done all my life. I must not offend my nobles, and I must do with your daughter as best I can. I must not please myself; I must please my people. But without your consent I will do nothing. But this I wish, that whatever I do, you will show that patience which you vowed to me you would preserve when we made our marriage in yonder village."

Griselda heard all this; and, though her heart was wrung with pain, yet she looked up with a countenance that was unmoved. Neither in her speech, nor in her manner did she seem to be in grief.

"My lord," she said, "my child and I are at your pleasure with hearty consent. We are wholly yours. Save or kill your own as it pleases you. There is nothing in all the wide world that will displease me if it please you. I desire to have nothing but you, and there is nothing that I would not willingly lose but you. This is the truth of my heart and nothing will ever change it."

Now when the marquis heard his wife speak thus loyally, he was glad in his heart; but he pretended not to be glad, and he went out of the chamber looking stern and cruel.

50   TALES OF CHIVALRY AND ROMANCE.

And after he had gone from the chamber, he called his trusty sergeant, and told him privately all his intentions towards his wife and his young daughter, and sent him to the marchioness. And when the sergeant knew well all that the marquis wished him to do, he stalked into the lady's chamber silently, like a murderer in the night.

"Madam," said he, "you must forgive me for doing a thing that I am commanded to do. You know well that the commands of the marquis must be executed. We may grieve and complain against them, but we must obey them. I am commanded to take this child."

He spoke no more, but roughly and cruelly snatched up the child in his hand, and began to make ready as if to slay it. Griselda had to suffer and consent. Meek and uncomplaining as a lamb she sits, and lets the cruel sergeant work his will. This sergeant was suspected of having done many dark deeds. His face had a suspicious look; he had come at a suspicious hour, and his words were dark and threatening. Oh, the young daughter that she loved so well! Griselda thought she was to be slain at once; but yet she neither wept nor sighed, but consented to the will of the marquis.

Then at last she spoke, and prayed the sergeant, as

THE PATIENT GRISELDA.

51

he was a worthy gentleman, to let her kiss her child before it died. She laid the little infant on her arm, and, with a sad, sad face, she blessed her, and murmured softly over her, and then began to kiss her.

"Farewell, my little one," she said, "I shall never see thee more. I pray Him that died upon the tree to bless thee. Thy soul, little child, I give to Him to keep, for surely this night must thou die for my sake."

Well might a mother at such a time as this have cried and bewailed aloud; but Griselda was so constant to her lord's commands that she endured all steadfastly. Then, turning to the sergeant, she meekly said :—

"Take here again this little, young maid. Go now and do my lord's will. But one thing I beseech of you, that, if my lord has not forbade it, you bury this little body in some place where no beasts or wild birds may tear it."

The sergeant said never a word, but went his way with the child.

Then the sergeant came to the marquis, and gave him the child, and told him all that Griselda had said and done. And when the lord heard what words his wife had spoken, and how submissively for his sake she had given up her infant, his heart melted, but he would not swerve from his purpose. He had a sister

52   TALES OF CHIVALRY AND ROMANCE.

who lived at Bologna, and was married to the Count of Panik there.   To her he desired the sergeant to take the little child safely, upon pain of death.   The sergeant was to wrap the little child in warm clothing, and to carry it tenderly to Bologna, telling no man whither he went nor whence he came, and was to beseech the Countess of Panik, the Marquis's sister, to foster the child and bring it up as her own daughter, but to conceal from every one whose child it was.

In all things the sergeant performed the orders of his sovereign.

But the marquis ?—He wonders if his wife will be changed in word or manner, but no change could he see.   She is still the same to him, steadfast, cheerful, obedient, and kind.   She is still humble, busy in her service, and in her love towards him, and moves about the palace with a happy face.   Never does she mention the name of her daughter, and she is cheerful, and even gay, as if she never had, or had never lost her child.

After four years had passed, Griselda had a son, a very beautiful child, and at his birth there was great rejoicing; for not only did the marquis rejoice and make merry, but all his people were glad that an heir had been born who would rule over them when the time should come for their ruler to die.   And when the

THE PATIENT GRISELDA. 53

boy was two years old the marquis bethought him that he would again try the constancy and obedience of his wife. Ah, surely her faithfulness had been tried abundantly! But the Lord of Saluce was stubborn in will, and he yielded to the temptation to put the patience of Griselda further to the proof.

"Wife," said he to Griselda, "you must have heard that my people look unkindly upon our marriage; and since my son was born they are worse pleased than ever. The murmuring of my subjects pierces my heart, and the noise of their displeasure has almost slain me. Thus say my people :—'When Walter is gone, then shall the base blood of Janicula, the peasant, rule over us; for there is no other heir.' Now I desire to live in peace; and so I wish to serve our little son by night as I did his sister. I will deal with him privately, as I dealt with our daughter. And now, I warn you, do not suddenly forget yourself! Be patient, I pray you."

Then said Griselda :—"I have ever said, and ever shall say that I will have nothing but what you please to let me have. It does not grieve me even though my daughter and my son be slain, if it be at your commandment. Ah me! all that I have had of my two children has been, first sickness and afterwards woe and pain. But you are our lord; we are your own.

54 TALES OF CHIVALRY AND ROMANCE.

Do with your own what pleaseth you. Ask no counsel from me; for as I left at home all my poor clothing when I first came to you, so I left also my will and my liberty. Do then your pleasure—I will obey. And surely had I known what was your wish, I would have striven to have pleased you before. If I thought that my death would ease you, right gladly would I die rather than displease you; for I hold death lightly compared with your love!"

And when the marquis heard these words, and knew the constancy of his wife, he cast down his eyes, and his heart was full of love for her. He wondered that she could endure the loss of her children; but still he held to his wish to try her further, and he went away from her with a lowering, unkind countenance, though in his heart he was happy.

Then, after a while, came in the ugly sergeant and, rudely as he had taken away her daughter, or even more rudely, he snatched away Griselda's young son, who was so beautiful. But still through all Griselda was patient. Her countenance was not sorrowful. She kissed and blessed the child, and let him go. One thing only she besought of the sergeant—that he would lay her little son in an earthen grave, so that no beasts or ravenous birds should harm his tender limbs. The sergeant made no promise, but secretly

THE PATIENT GRISELDA. 55

carried the boy to Bologna, where his sister was now staying.

And ever the marquis wonders more and more at the patience of Griselda. Had he not known with certainty that she loved her children most dearly, he would have thought that there was some evil or cruel hardiness in his wife's nature; for still, after losing both her children, she maintained a calm and cheerful face, and an uncomplaining mien. But the marquis well knew that, after himself, Griselda loved her children more than all the world. And why then will he try her truth further? Surely he has had proof enough of her obedience. But there are some people who when they have taken up a certain purpose will follow it out to the end, and of this temper was the Lord of Saluce. He watched Griselda, but neither in word, deed, nor look was she in any way changed towards him. In her heart she loved her husband above all, and her face showed what was in her heart, and was full of affection. The longer she stayed with him, the more truly devoted she became to him, if that were possible.

Nothing is now ever heard of the two children. No one but the marquis and his sergeant knew that they were safe at Bologna. The people of Saluce thought that the marquis had murdered them because their

56 TALES OF CHIVALRY AND ROMANCE.

mother had been a poor woman ; and, instead of loving him as they had done, they began to hate him for his cruelty ; but the hatred of his subjects did not alter the purpose of the marquis, or soften his determination. He was firmly fixed upon tempting his wife still further.

So when his daughter was twelve years old the marquis sent privately to the court of Rome, desiring his friends there to frame a dispensation as if from the Pope, giving him liberty to put away his wife and marry another. This false dispensation was made, and it was sealed, to all appearance, with the Pope's seal. It set forth that the Marquis of Saluce, having married a poor woman, and having thus kindled the wrath of his subjects, was at liberty to forsake his present wife, and, by marrying a noble lady, try to win back the love of his people. The marquis had this matter so cunningly devised, that all his rude and ignorant subjects believed that it was a real dispensation from the Pope that had been sent. When the tidings were told to Griselda, her heart was full of woe ; but she bore her grief with a calm face, and in her sweet humility and constancy she set herself to endure all the adversity of her fortune.

Then the marquis wrote a letter and sent it secretly to the Count of Panik, the husband of his sister. In

THE PATIENT GRISELDA.

the letter he prayed the Count of Panik to bring his two children back to Saluce with all state and honourable ceremony; not to tell whose children they were to any man, but to say that the young fair maiden was going away to be married to the Marquis of Saluce. The count did as the marquis desired; and on a certain day he set out on his way to Saluce, with many lords and ladies in his train, and with Griselda's daughter and young son, and all their attendants. The maiden was attired as for her marriage, and her garment glistened with gems. Her brother, who was now seven years old, was also richly and splendidly clothed. With great pomp and with glad cheer, this noble company march from day to day towards Saluce.

Still was the marquis determined to test the steadfastness of his wife to the very uttermost, and with this intent he one day spoke to her thus roughly before all his lords :—

"Truly, Griselda," said he, "in having you for my wife, I have been fortunate in finding you good, and true, and obedient, but not so fortunate in finding you either rich or of ancient lineage. I have learned in sober sadness that sovereignty is but another name for service, and that a king is less free than the meanest of his subjects. My people beseech me every day to take another wife, and the Pope has commanded

58 TALES OF CHIVALRY AND ROMANCE.

me to put you from me and wed another, in order that peace and content may be restored throughout the land. And, indeed, already my young bride is on her way to Saluce. Command your feelings, and give way and make room for the new comer! And the dowry that you brought, take it again, and return to your father's house. With bold heart bear this accident of fortune! Lasting prosperity is the lot of no mortal!"

Then answered the patient Griselda, with breaking heart, but with calm countenance:—

"My lord, I know, and have always known, that between your magnificence and my poverty there is no comparison or seemliness, and that I have never been worthy to be your wife. You made me the lady of this palace; but I have never borne me as its mistress. I have ever been your servant in meekness and humility, and ever shall be until I die. I thank heaven and you, that in your kindness you have so long entertained me in honour and nobility; and I pray that all your goodness to me will be repaid to you. For me, I will gladly go to my father's house, and live with him till the end of my days. There was I reared as a little child, and there will I die. May you have all happiness and prosperity with your new wife! Gladly will I yield her my place in which I

THE PATIENT GRISELDA. 59

have lived so many blissful years ; for it is your will that I should go from the place of my heart's rest. You offer me the dowry that I brought to you when first I came ; but I only brought wretched clothes, and now, after so long, it will be hard to find them. Oh, my heart! how kind and gentle you seemed in word and in manner on that day when first our marriage was made! Ah! truly is it said, and I have bitter proof of it, that love is sweet when it is new, but when it is old, it loses its sweet savour. But, my lord, no pang, no adversity will ever make me repent that I gave my whole heart to you. You know that in my father's dwelling you bade me leave my poor clothing, when in your kindness you clad me in marriage robes. Here, again, I restore you my garments and my wedding ring. The jewels that you gave me I have left in your chamber. Naked I came from my father's house, and naked will I return there again! Yet, my lord, you surely will not send me from your palace without a covering! You could not do so discourteous a thing. Let me not go forth among your people like a worm. Oh, remember, my own lord so dear! I was your wife, though not worthy of you. Here, now, lest I grieve you, I bid you farewell, my own lord."

Then the marquis assented that she should keep a part of her clothing on to cover her. But scarcely could he speak the words, so full was his heart of love and pity.

Before all the people, the meek Griselda took off all her costly garments, and then, with bare head and

bare feet, and but scantily covered, she set forth towards her father's house.

And as she went forth from the palace, the people followed her, bewailing the great evil that had fallen

THE PATIENT GRISELDA. 61

upon her, and weeping to see all her sadness and humility. But she kept her eyes dry from weeping, nor ever spoke a word against her bitter fate. Her father, hearing the noise of the people as they came towards his house loudly mourning, and seeing Griselda coming towards him almost naked, cursed the day that he was born; for the poor old man had ever thought that the happiness of his daughter with the marquis would last but a little time, and that as soon as the Lord of Saluce began to tire of her, he would remember her humble birth and put her from him. The old man went hastily to his daughter, and bitterly weeping for pity, he covered her nakedness with the old coat which she had left behind her when she was dressed in her costly marriage robes, and led her to his house.

Now Griselda, this flower of womanly patience, dwelt with her father in their lowly hut. Never did she complain, or show by word or look, either before the people or when alone, that any offence had been done to her. In her prosperity she was ever humble, showing no love of dainties, no pomp, no pride, but bearing herself with patient benignity, discretion, and honour, and with meekness and constancy to her husband, to whom she knew she owed all that she enjoyed. And in her adversity she was still as steadfast and unmoved by her changed fortune. No man can

62 TALES OF CHIVALRY AND ROMANCE.

bear himself in humbleness as a woman, or can be half so true.

Soon it was known that the Count of Panik had come to Saluce from Bologna, and all the people had heard that he had brought with him a young wife for the marquis with such pomp and splendour as had never before been seen in all Lombardy. The marquis, wishing his palace to be made ready to receive the strangers, sent for Griselda. Poor Griselda, not knowing that the hardest trial of all was in store for her, came with humble heart and willing mind, and bending down on her knees, she greeted the marquis with reverence and kindness.

"Griselda," said he, "it is my will that this maiden to whom I am to be wedded shall be received in my house to-morrow with all royalty, and also that every knight and squire that comes in her service shall be received and lodged according to his estate and degree. There is no woman here to make ready the chambers as I wish them, and therefore I desire you to take this charge upon yourself. Your dress is so bad that you can hardly be seen; but do your best in this matter."

"I am glad, my lord," said Griselda, "to do your pleasure, and I desire to serve and please you, without weariness, in all that one so humble may. I shall ever love you best, with all truth, come weal or woe!"

THE PATIENT GRISELDA. 63

Then began Griselda to prepare the house for the coming of the bride—to make the beds, to set the tables, and to order the servants of the household in all their sweeping and cleaning, until every chamber and hall was ready.

And at the sinking of the sun came this Count of Panik, with the two noble children, the son and daughter of the marquis and Griselda. The people ran to see the young maiden that had come to be married, as they thought, to their lord.

"Our marquis is no fool," said they; "for though it has seemed good to him to change his wife, it is all for the best. This damsel is fairer than Griselda, of more tender years, and is of noble parentage."

O stormy people! Fickle, and ever untrue; foolish and changeful as the church vane that swings and turns to every breeze. You place your delight on whatever is new, you change like the moon, your judgment is false, your constancy is ever failing, and the man is a fool that places dependence upon you!

Meantime Griselda is busy every hour of the day with the matters belonging to the marriage feast. She was not ashamed of her clothing, though it was rude and coarse and torn in many places, but went forth with the other people of the household to the gate of the palace to greet the new marchioness. Then she

64 TALES OF CHIVALRY AND ROMANCE.

received the guests and bestowed them in chambers suitable to their rank, so wisely and discreetly that all of them were pleased; and, though they wondered at her poor attire, they extolled her prudence. She praised the maiden and her young brother with all her heart, though she believed that the maid had come to be the wife, and to win all the love, of the marquis.

When all the lords had assembled in the great hall where a masque was being performed, the marquis called Griselda, who was busy among the guests, to his side.

"Griselda," said he, gaily, as if in the fulness of his joy and pride, "how does my wife and her beauty please you?"

"Right well, my lord," answered Griselda, in her sincerity; "for, in good truth, I have never seen a fairer than she. I pray to God to give her prosperity, and I hope that He will send you both happiness till the end of your days. One thing I warn you and beseech of you. Hurt not this tender maiden with tormentings and with great sorrows, as you have done me, for she has been fostered tenderly, and could not endure adversity as could a creature poorly fostered."

When the marquis now witnessed her great patience, her cheerful submission, and her faithful, uncomplain-

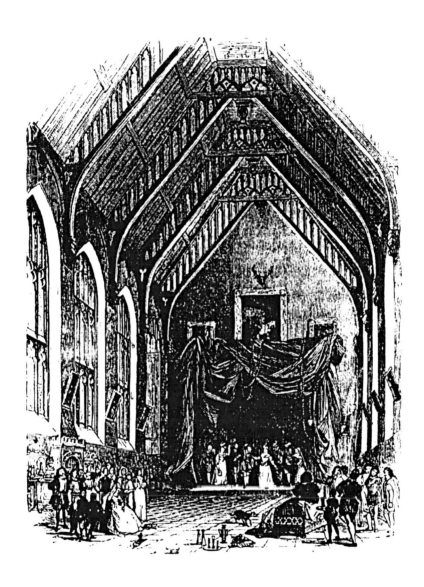

When all the lords had assembled in the great hall, where a masque was being performed, the marquis called Griselda, who was busy among the guests, to his side.

66   TALES OF CHIVALRY AND ROMANCE.

ing love, after all the miseries and sorrows she had undergone,—when he saw her still innocent, tender, and true,—his whole heart went out towards her.

"This is enough, my Griselda," said the marquis. "Fear no more, cast your sorrows aside, you have had enough of evil. In faith and in worthiness, you have been tried more than ever woman was. Now, my dear wife, I know your steadfastness." And he took her in his arms and kissed her.

But she wondering, and stupefied at the words she had heard, gazed about her in fear, like one that has started out of sleep.

"You are my own wife, Griselda; none other have I had or ever will have. This is our daughter whom you suppose to be my bride; this is our little son, who shall be my heir. You are their true mother. I have kept them long from you at Bologna. Take them now again, for, as you may see, you have lost neither of your children. And I now tell all people, whatever they may have said of me, that I have done this out of no malice or cruelty. Heaven forbid that I should seek to slay my children. I took them from my wife only that I might prove her true womanhood and faithfulness to me."

When Griselda heard this she swooned away for very joy, and afterwards, weeping fast tears, she took

THE PATIENT GRISELDA. 67

her children in her arms and embraced them with all her mother's love, and kissed them tenderly. Oh, it was pitiful to see her swooning, and then to hear her low voice as, weeping, she said :—

"God give you thanks, my lord, for saving my dear children! Now would I willingly die here at this moment ; for since you have given me again your love and your grace, I care not how soon I die! Oh, my tender, dear, young children, your woeful mother long believed that cruel beasts had devoured you, but God, in his mercy, and your father, have given you back to me as from the grave."

Then, suddenly fainting, she fell to the ground, and lay as dead, still clasping her children to her bosom in such a close embrace that the marquis could hardly raise them from her arms, while the fast-falling tears ran down the faces of all that stood around. Afterwards the marquis, soothing her and comforting her, raised her from her trance till she opened her eyes and began to speak again. And a while after she awoke, the ladies of the palace went with her into a chamber, and taking off her rude clothes, arrayed her in a shining robe of cloth of gold, and placed on her head a crown enriched with many a precious stone, and brought her into the hall again, where all the lords paid her the homage which was her due.

Thus this mournful day had a joyous ending, and every one in the palace spent the hours in mirth and feasting till the stars shone out brightly from the front of the sky. And, long after, it was said that this feast was even more solemn and splendid than the revelry of the day of Griselda's marriage.

The marquis and Griselda lived happily for many a year, and Janicula, the patient lady's father, came also and dwelt in the palace until he died. After the marquis died his son succeeded him to the throne, and reigned prosperously and happily, while his daughter was married to one of the worthiest lords in all the country.

Griselda is dead, and her patience is buried with her in Italy; but her story is still told to teach us, every one in his degree, to bear adversity with constancy and with uncomplaining humility.

This is the end of this publication.

Any remaining blank pages are for our book binding
requirements and are blank on purpose.

To search thousands of interesting publications like this one,
please remember to visit our website at:

http://www.kessinger.net

CPSIA information can be obtained at www.ICGtesting.com
Printed in the USA
BVOW03s1437281014

372680BV00028B/534/P